1

The First People saw many large
birds.

3

There were birds that swam in the sea.

Ducks were caught on the lakes and rivers.

Big eggs were a good form of food.

9

Feathers of the galah were used in dance.

11

The First People used bird feathers. The feathers were used for dance and music.

13

Birds were totems to the First People. Totems were their helping spirits.

15

Big birds like the emu were food for the First People.

17

Mutton birds were a good food for people near the coast.

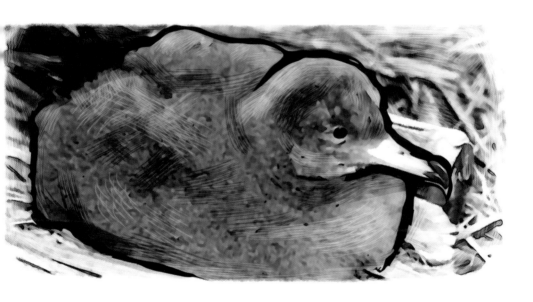

The Wedgetail Eagle was a very big bird. It was a totem to some of the First People.

Birds were a totem to many of the First People.

23

Word bank

spirits

totems

dance

feathers

food

form

large

birds

swam

ducks

lakes

rivers

dance

music

helping

mutton

people